Catchwords Yellow
Charles Cripps

Third Edition

illustrated by Allan Stomann,
Katrina van Gendt
and Philip Eldridge

HBJ Harcourt Brace Jovanovich, Publishers
London   Sydney   Orlando   Toronto

UK edition published by
Harcourt Brace Jovanovich Limited
24/28 Oval Road, London NW1 7DX

Copyright © 1990, 1988, 1983, 1978 by
Harcourt Brace Jovanovich
Group (Australia) Pty Limited

This publication is copyright. Except as expressly provided in the Copyright Act 1968, no part of this publication may be reproduced by any means (including electronic, mechanical, microcopying, photocopying, recording or otherwise) without prior written permission from the publisher.

Printed in Australia

ISBN 0 7466 0021 6

When learning to spell these words you must always:—

LOOK
Look carefully at the word so that you remember what you have seen.

COVER
Cover the word with the flap.

WRITE
Write the word from memory.

CHECK
Lift the flap and check that you have written the word correctly.

If you have not written the word correctly start again. Look at the word. Cover it and write it from memory. Then check your spelling.

1 Write the word **at** on each cat, and then on each picture.

Write each word on a step of the ladder.

b____
c____
h____
s____
p____
f____
r____

Draw a line from the word to the picture.

2 Write the word **it** on each sock.

Now make some new words beginning with the letters on the legs.

3 Write the letter **i** on the washing to make words.

4 Write the **ot** letter pattern on each teapot.

Now make some new words.

n

ot

g

l

h

....

....

....

....

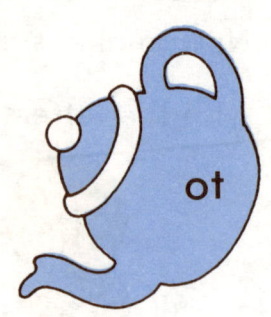

5 Write the letter **o** on each kite.

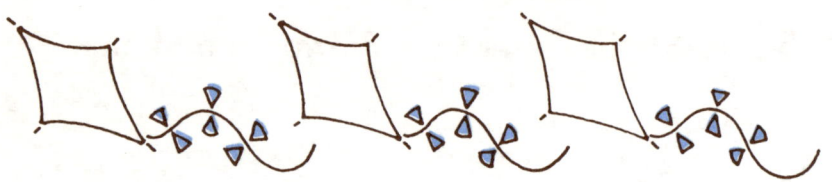

Now make some new words with the letters on the tail.

o

g

s

wh

n

d

t

....

....

....

....

....

6 Use red to fill in this letter pattern.

ut

Now do the same in each word.

cut
but hut
put

Look at the letter pattern and write the words.

....

....

....

7 Write the word **hat** on each hat.

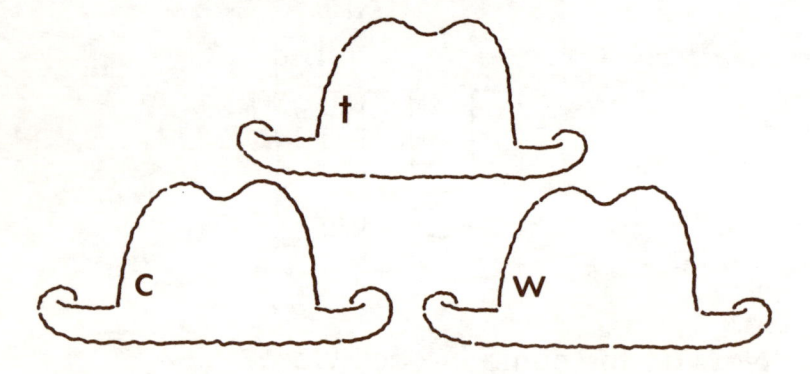

t

c   w

Now write these words.

t _____

c _____

w _____

8 Post the letters in the right letter boxes.

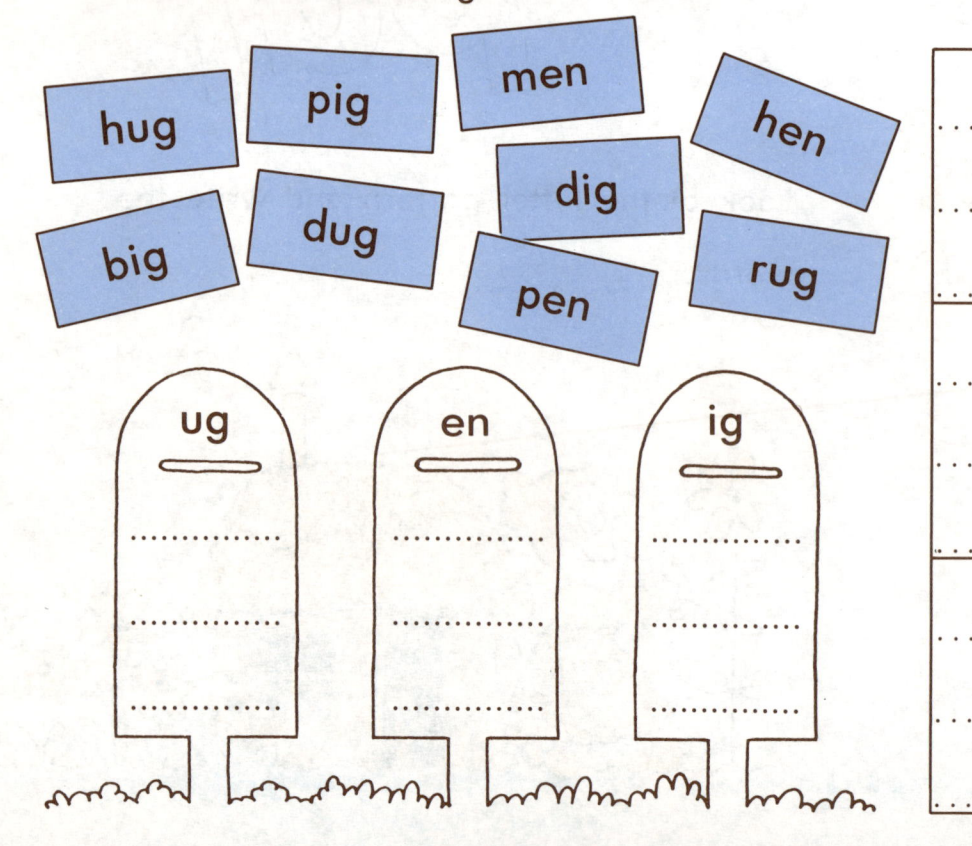

hug   pig   men   hen
big   dug   dig   rug
      pen

ug   en   ig

9 Write the **et** letter pattern on each jet.

Now make some new words.

m
l
j
w
n
p

et

10 Add **up** to these letters to make new words.

c ____

p ____

Add **e** to these letters to make new words.

h ____

m ____

w ____

b ____

sh ____

11 Write the **op** letter pattern on each top.

Now make some new words.

....

....

....

....

12 Write the word **an** on each fan.

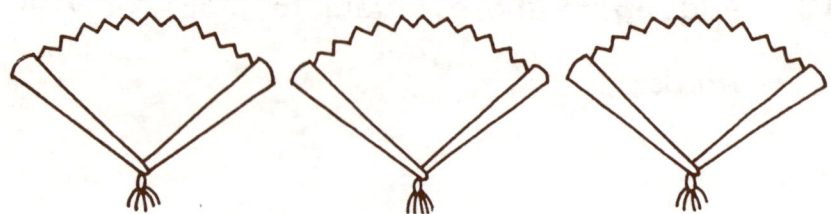

Write this word on each step of the ladder.

....

....

....

....

Draw a line from the word to the picture.

13 Look at these words.

They all have the same letter pattern.

    fun   **run**   **gun**   **sun**

Now step across the river by writing each word on a stone.

14 Write the **ap** letter pattern on each cap.

Now make some new words beginning with the letters in the balloons.

15 Write the **ad** letter pattern on each pad.

Now make some new words.

s, b, m, h, gl — ad

....

....

....

....

....

16 Write the **ag** letter pattern on each bag.

Now make some new words beginning with the letters on the dogs.

b, r, w — ag

....

....

....

17 Write the **um** letter pattern on each drum.

Now make some new words beginning with the letters in the circles.

g — um
h — um
dr — um

....
....
....

18 Look at the word on the roof.

Find the words with this letter pattern and write them on the house.

they   **the**   three
these   them
there   this
those   then

....
....
....
....

19 Use green to fill in the letter pattern.

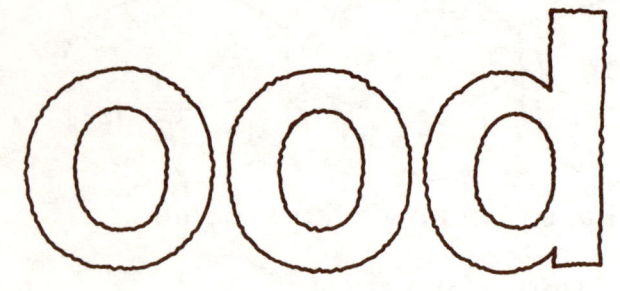

ood

Now do the same in each word.

good
wood
food

Look at the letter pattern and finish these words.

g _____

w _____

f _____

20 Look at these words.

They all have the same letter pattern.

red **bed** **fed** **led**

Now walk across the road by writing each word on the crossing.

21 Write the letter pattern **ip** on each ship.

Now make some new words beginning with the letters on the fish.

22 Write the **ing** letter pattern on each wing.

r
w
s
th
br
ing

....

....

....

....

....

23 Look at the **ong** letter pattern.

Find the way to the words with the same letter pattern.

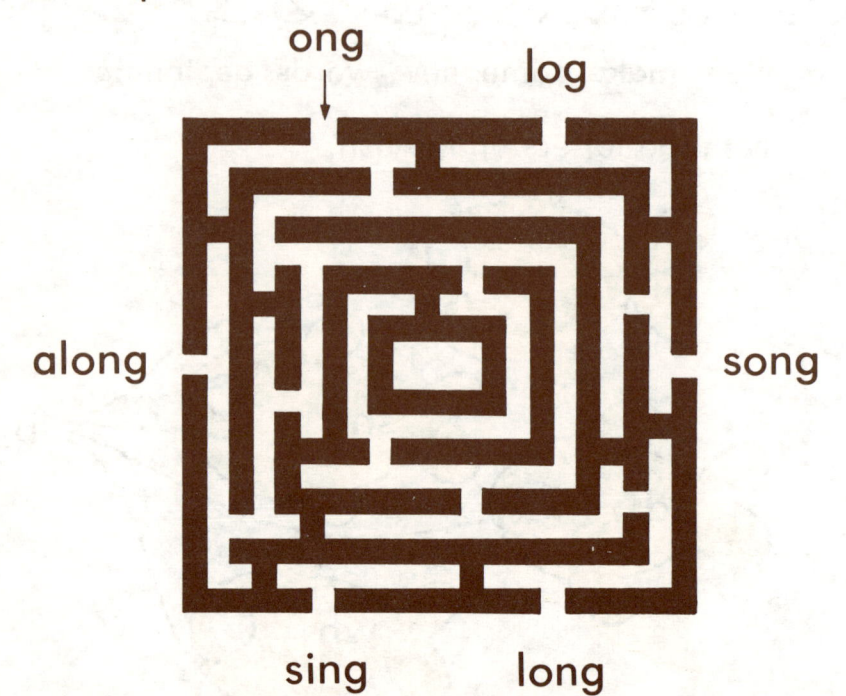

ong
log
along
song
sing   long

....

....

....

24 Write the **wi** letter pattern on each star.

Now make some new words.

wi — ll
wi — sh
wi — th

25 Write the **est** letter pattern on each nest.

Now make some new words beginning with the letters on the birds.

n b
r w
est

26 Write the **ent** letter pattern on each tent.

Now make some new words.

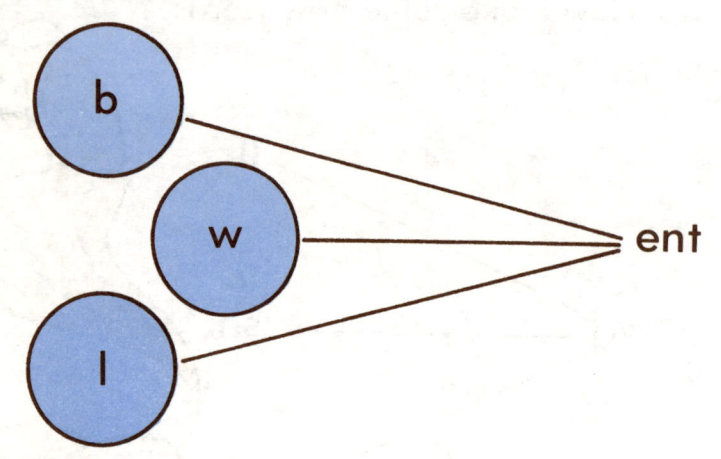

b → ent
w → ent
l → ent

....
....
....

27 Look at the word in the box and use the letter pattern to make new words.

Use crayons to finish the picture.

b**ell**

t _____
s _____
f _____
w _____

....
....
....
....

28 Write the **ind** letter pattern on each tree.

Now make some new words.

....

....

....

29 Look at the word in the hill and use the letter pattern to make new words.

hill

....

....

....

w _____   t _____   m _____

30 Use red to fill in this letter pattern.

hi

Now do the same in each word.

hill
him his

Look at the letter pattern and write the words.

....
....
....

31 Write the **ost** letter pattern on each purse.

Now make some new words.

c
l
m
ost

....
....
....

32 Look at the letter pattern in the haystack.

Find the words with this letter pattern and write them in the haystack.

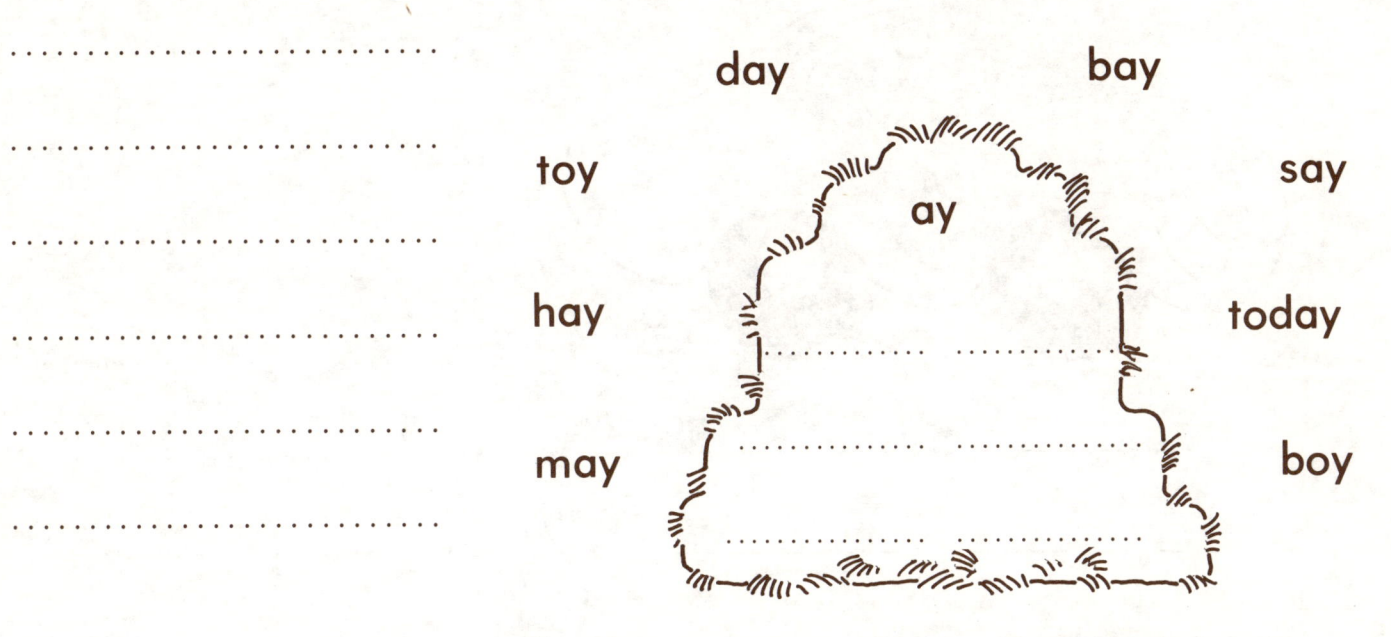

day   bay

toy   ay   say

hay   today

may   boy

33 Write the letter pattern **ee** on each tree.

Now make some new words.

s

tr   thr   ee

34 Look at the word on the car and use the letter pattern to make new words.

Use crayons to finish the picture.

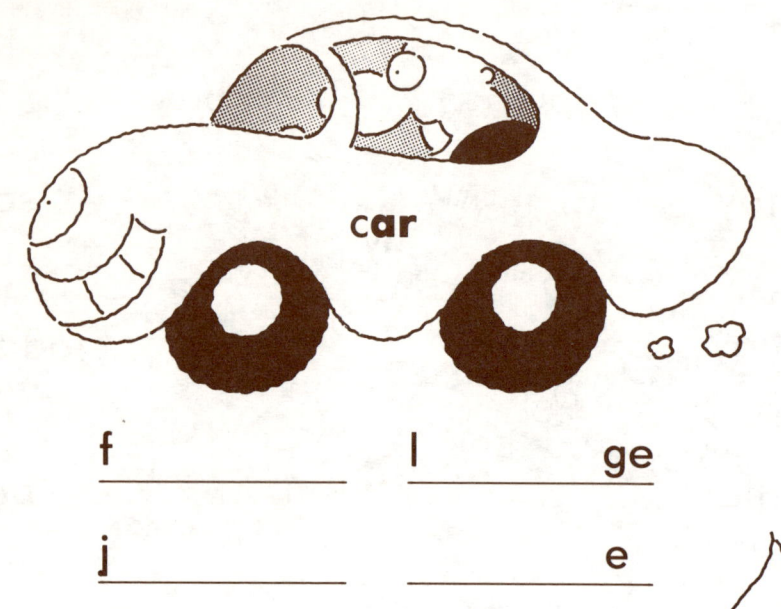

car

f _____   l _____ ge

j _____   _____ e

....

....

....

....

35 Add **ow** to make new words.

h _____

c _____

n _____

kn _____

....

....

....

....

36 Write the **ive** letter pattern on each hive.

Now make some new words.

f _____

g _____

g _____ s

l _____

....

....

....

....

37 Write the **ake** letter pattern on each cake.

Now make some new words.

c _____

m _____

m _____ s

t _____

t _____ s

....

....

....

....

38 Post the letters in the right letter boxes.

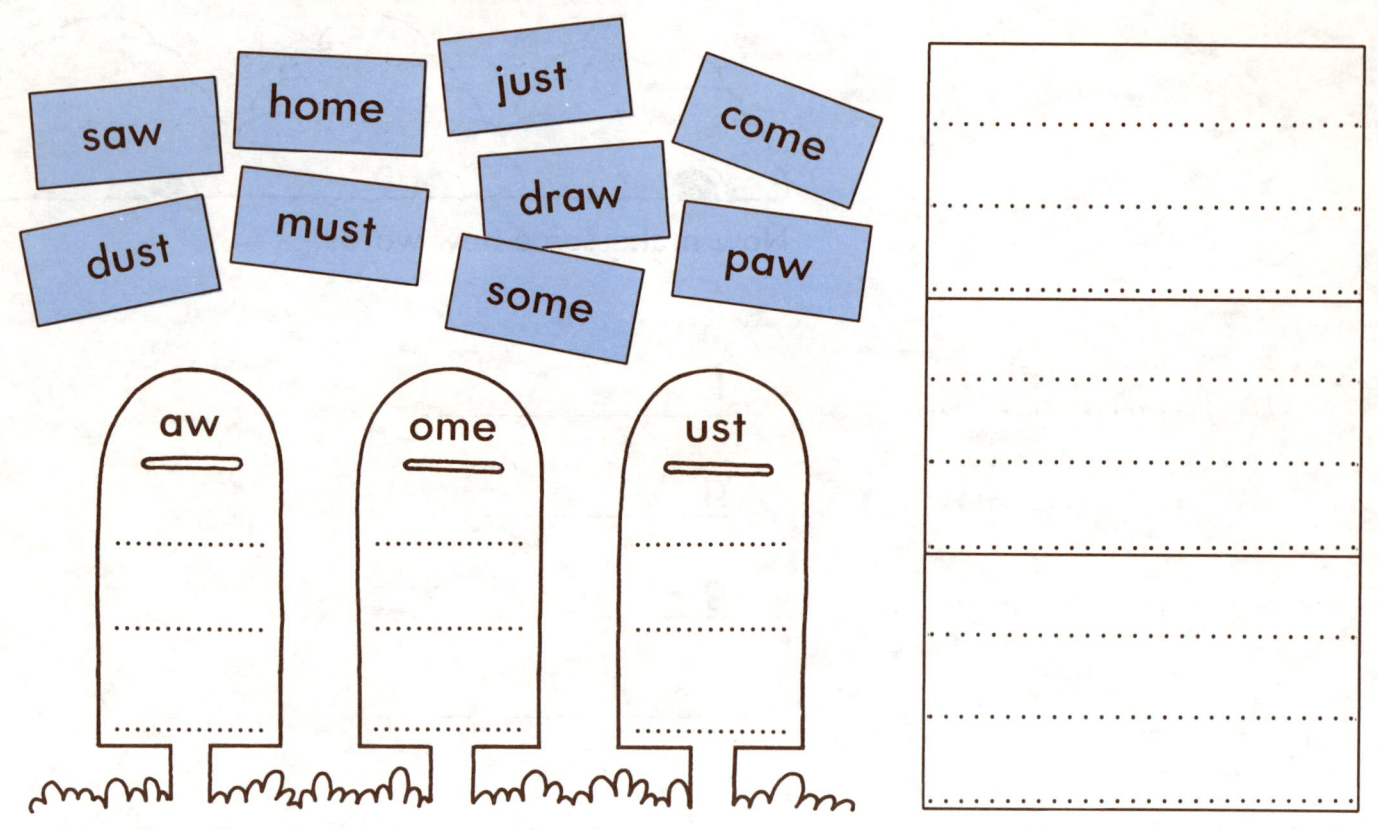

Words: saw, home, just, come, dust, must, draw, paw, some

Boxes: aw — ome — ust

39 Look at the **ame** letter pattern.

Find the way to the words with the same letter pattern.

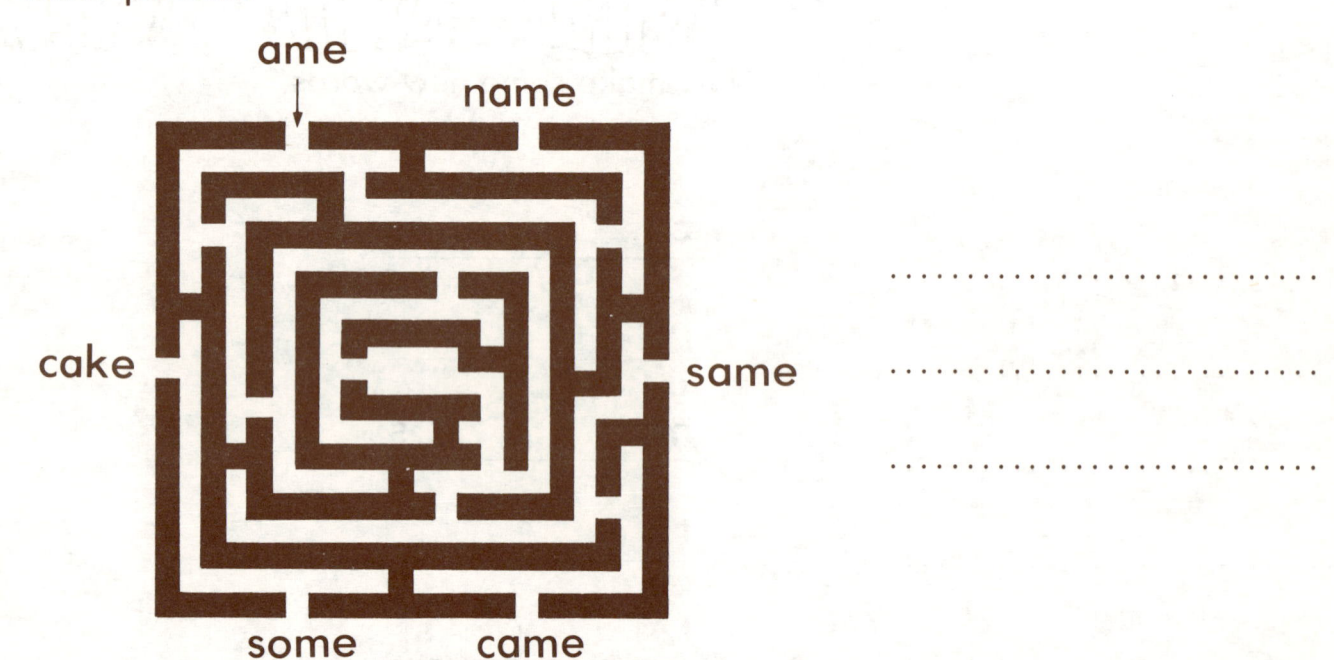

ame

name

cake   same

some   came

40 Write the word **all** on each ball.

Write this word on each step of the ladder.

b
f
c
t
w

Draw a line from the picture to the word.

41 Write the letter pattern **ook** on each book.

Now make some new words.

b _____
b _____ s
l _____
l _____ ing
l _____ ed
t _____

42 Write the word **as** on each basket.

Now make some new words beginning with the letters on the cherries.

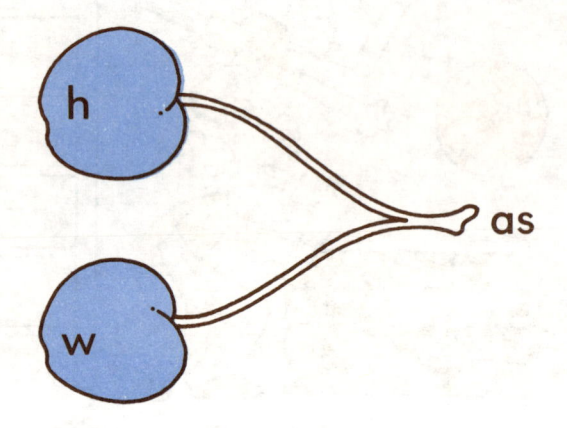

h — as
w

43 Trace over the lines to find the word pairs.

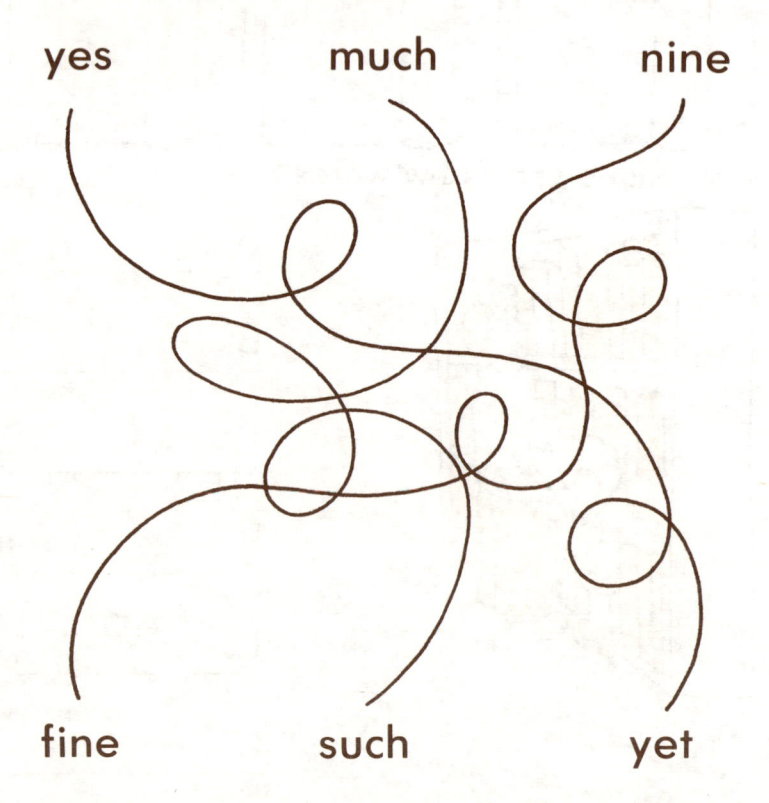

yes   much   nine

fine   such   yet

44 Many words look like other words.

Find these words and write them down.

a fox in a box

a jar **of ja**m

a dog **on a l**og

a hot **sp**ot

a happ**y app**le

45 Write the letter **y** on each kite.

Now make some new words with the letters on the tail.

46 Look at the word **her**.

Now use it to make new words.

t _____ e

w _____ e

_____ e

47 Can you use the picture to find the story?

Write out each story.

hereisthedog

....

whereismycat?

....

theballisunderthetree

....

puttheboxonthetable

....

mydadhasabigcar

....

48 Change a **he**
into a s**he**.
Now change a **he**
into a **he**r

Put **her**
over **her**e
and then
change **her**
from **her**e
to t**her**e.

he
+ he
= they

49 Look at the word **old**.

Now use it to make new words.

c _____ ....

t _____ ....

f _____ ....

50 Look at the word **eat**.

Now use it to make new words.

s _____ ....

m _____ ....

51 Look at the word **ear**.

Now use it to make new words.

d _____ ....

y _____ ....

h _____ ....

52 Draw a line between each word pair.

roof   b**een**

p**oor**

s**leep**   k**eep**

gr**een**

d**oor**   **roo**m

Now write the word pairs.

53 Look at the word **here.**

here

Now use it to make new words.

t _____

w _____

54 Write the word **ace** on each face.

Now use this word to finish writing the word on each step of the ladder.

f
l
r
sp
pl

Draw a line from the word to the picture.

55 Write the word **our** on each jug.

Now make some new words beginning with the letters in the circles.

f
y
our

56 Trace over the lines to find the word pairs.

frog　　　out　　　said

our　　　sail　　　from

57 Write the **ere** letter pattern on each clown.

Now make some new words beginning with the letters on the signs.

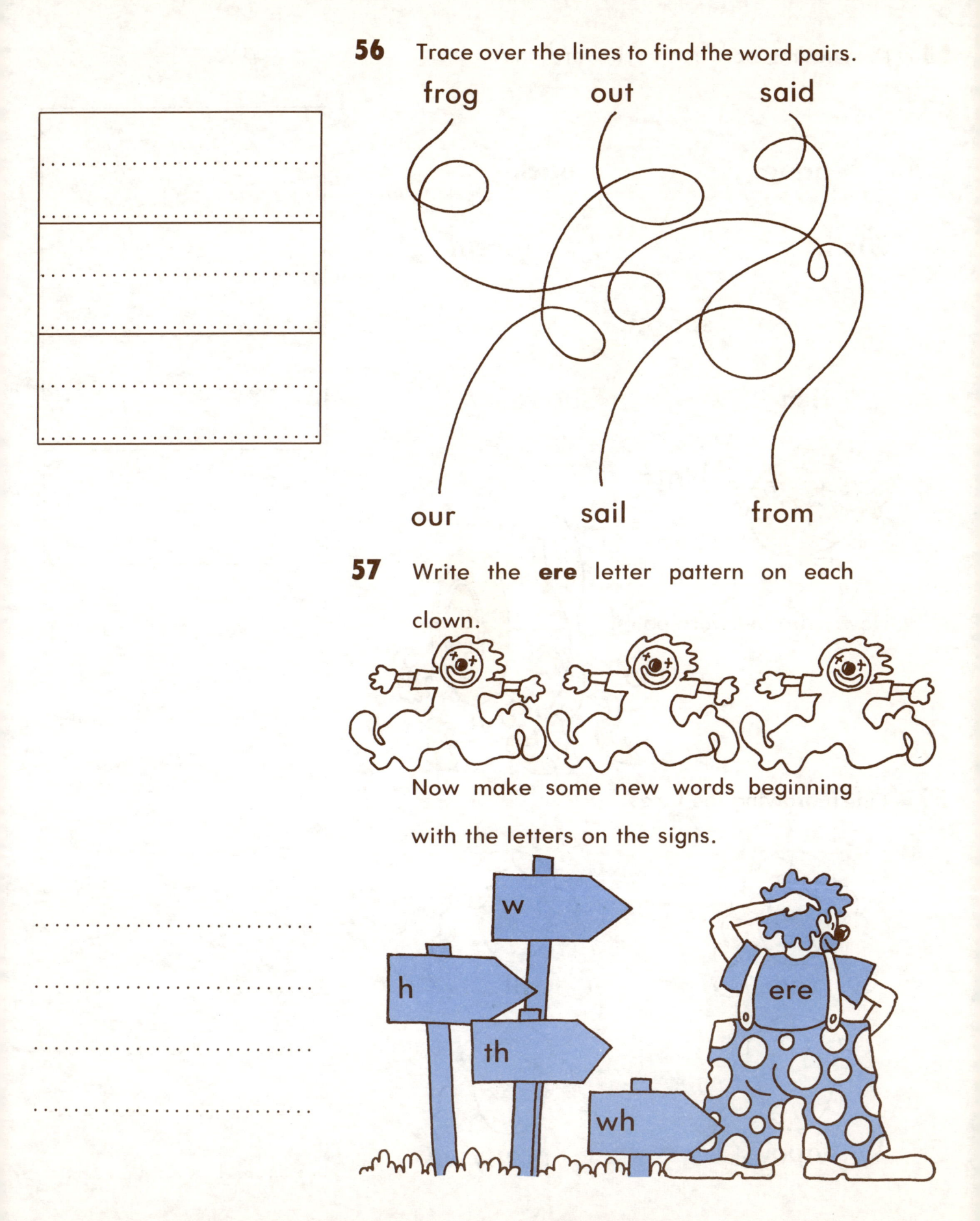

58 Draw a line between each word pair.

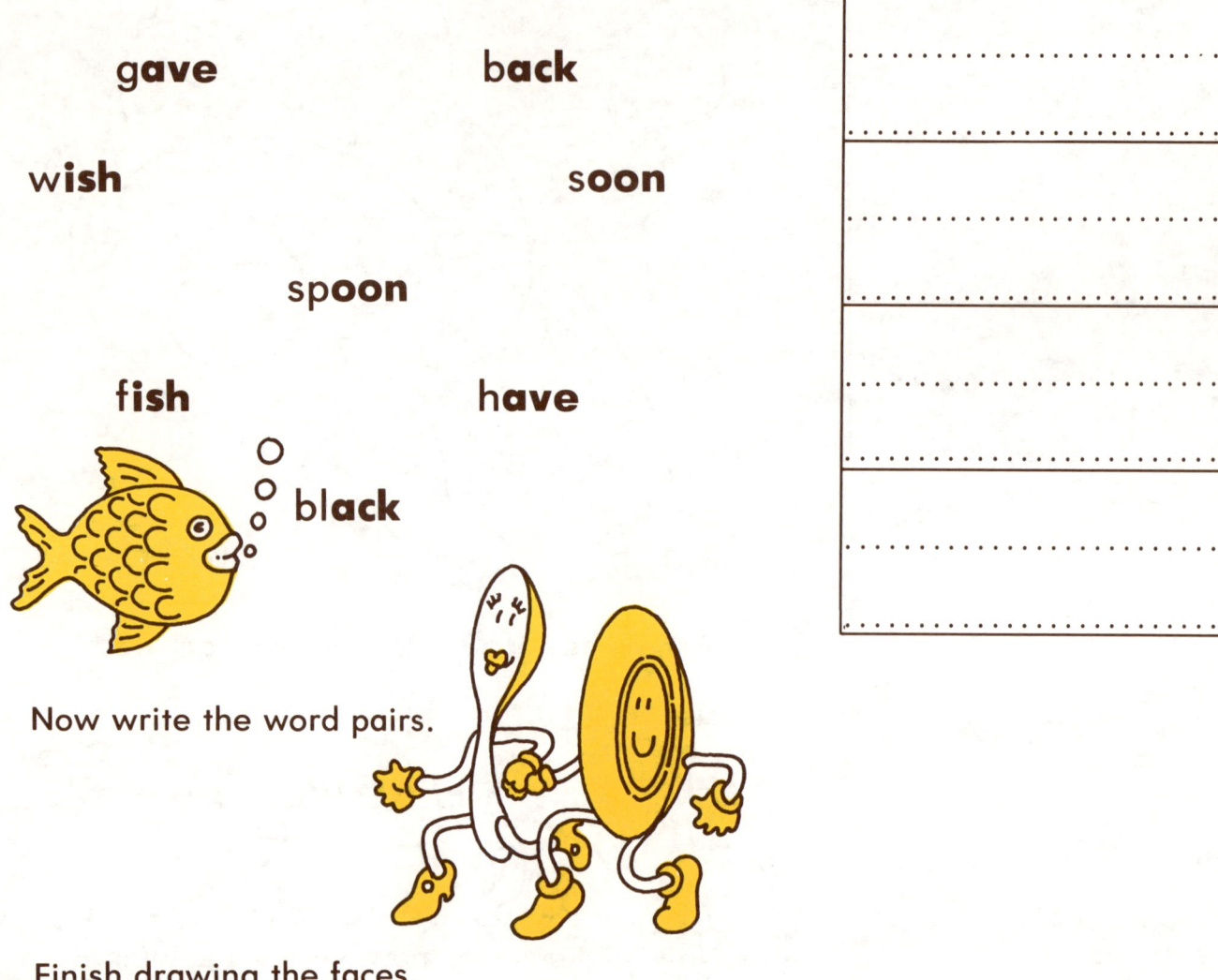

gave   back

wish   soon

    spoon

 fish   have

        black

Now write the word pairs.

59 Finish drawing the faces.

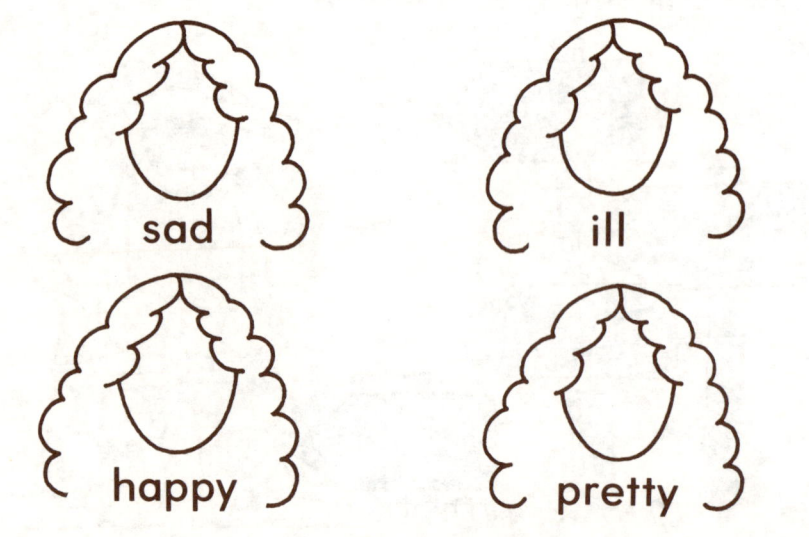

sad   ill

happy   pretty

60 Look at each word and use it to make new words.

own
- d _____
- t _____

ever
- _____ y
- n _____

an
- _____ y
- m _____ y

61 Look carefully at **out.**

Now try to write **about.**

Now do the same for the following.

he   head
now   know
ice   nice
lose   close
end   friend

62 Trace over the lines to find the word pairs.

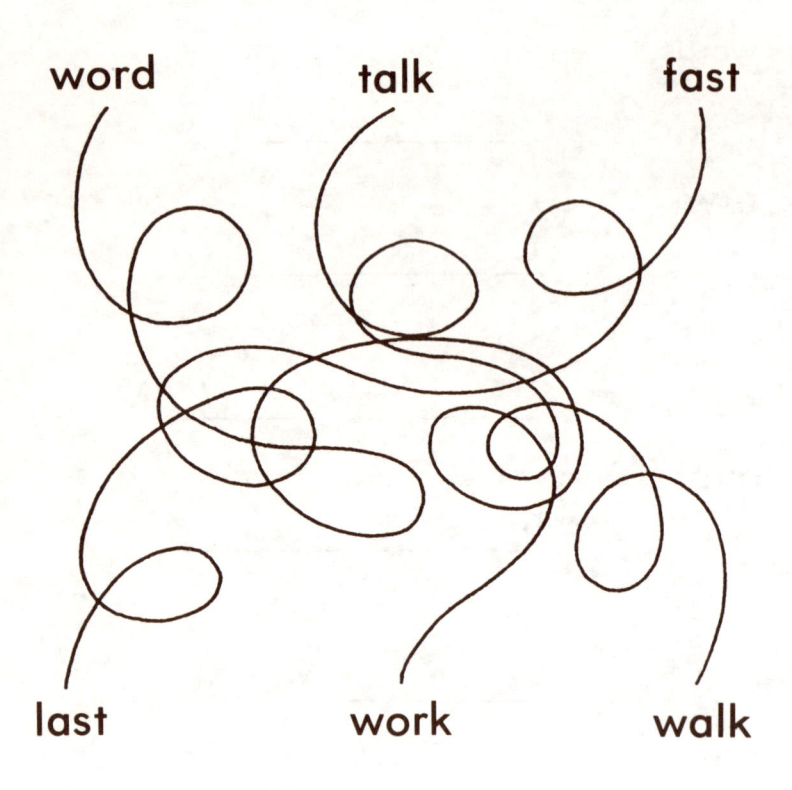

word   talk   fast

last   work   walk

63 Write the **ir** letter pattern on each bird.

Now make some new words.

b___   d___

g___   l___

f___   ___st

64 Look at the word **other.**

other

Now use it to make new words.

m _____

m _____ s

br _____

br _____ s

_____ s

an _____

65 Look at the word **thin.**

thin

Now use it to make new words.

_____ k

_____ ks

_____ g

_____ gs

no _____ g

some _____ g

66 Draw a line between each word pair.

wh**ite**   d**oing**

wh**ere**   w**ater**

l**ater**   wr**ite**

w**ere**   g**oing**

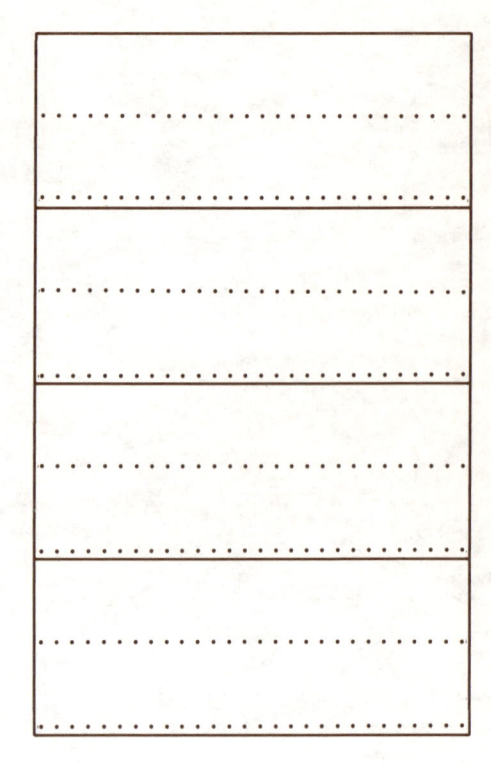

Now write each word pair.

67 Write the **wh** letter pattern on each truck.

Now make some new words ending with the letters on the dogs.

68 Write the **ue** letter pattern on each cloud.

Now make some new words beginning with the letters in the boxes.

bl
gl — ue
tr

....

....

....

69 Look at the letter pattern in each box and use it to make new words.

cr
tr — y

th
wh — en

b
t — oy

....

....

....

....

....

70 Can you use the picture to find the story?

Write out each story.

pleasegivemysistertheegg

....

myfatherlivesinthathouse

....

mybrotherhasalittleboat

....

thegirlreadstoherfriend

....

71 Look carefully at **end**.

Now try to write **friend**.   ....

Now do the same for the following.

child	children
use	because
very	every
you	your
hear	heard

....

....

....

....

....

72 Find the word families and write them in the boxes.

love
come
like
loves
likes
comes
loving
liking
coming

73 Look at each letter pattern and use it to make new words.

ore

ove

ter

m_____
bef_____
_____r
l_____
sis_____
af_____

74 Look at the **ould** letter pattern.

Find the way to the words with the same letter pattern.

ould
cold
fold
would
should
could

....

....

....

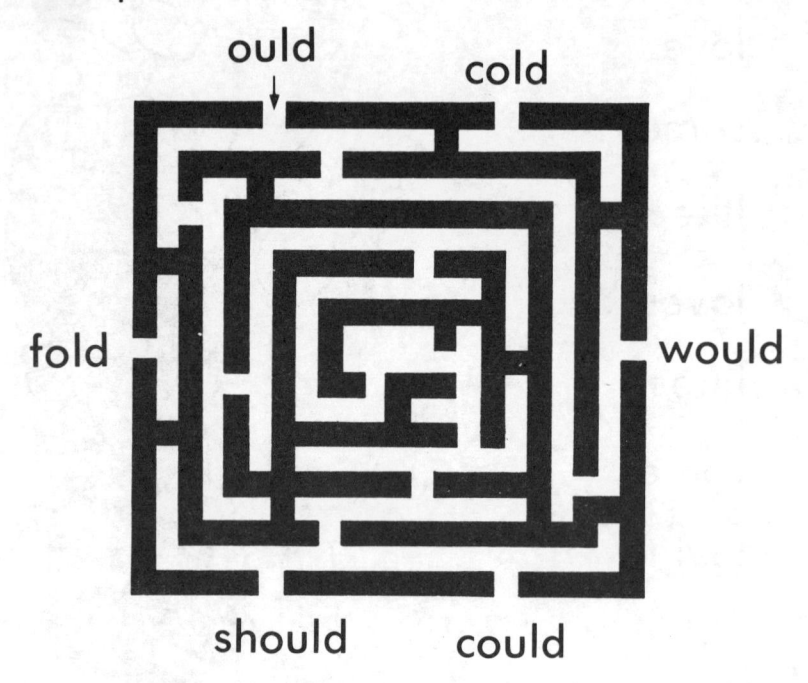

75 Look at the **ound** letter pattern.

Find the way to the words with the same letter pattern.

ound
kind
count
round
around
found

....

....

....

76 Write the **ain** letter pattern on each train.

Now make some new words.

tr —
r —— ain
ag —

....
....
....

77 Find the word families and write them in the boxes.

ask

work

want

worked

asks

wants

works

wanted

asked

78 Look at each word.

Draw a picture and write each word.

road   people

....

....

....

school   rabbit

....

....

....

street   picture

79 Look at each word and use it to make new words.

each

t _____

t _____ er

....

....

thing

some _____

no _____

....

an

_____ y

m _____ y

....

....

80 Draw a line between each word pair.

th**rough**   r**ight**

n**ew**   th**ough**t

d**inner**   f**ew**

n**ight**   w**inner**

Now write each word pair.

81 Look at the letter pattern in each box and use it to make words.

tw — o / enty

un — til / der

mi — lk / nd

ma — de / ke

82 Look carefully at the following words.

money

time

left

week

buy

Answer each question by writing the correct word.

Write the word ending in **me**. ....

Write the word with **one** in the middle. ....

Write the word beginning with **bu**. ....

Write the word with **ee** in the middle. ....

Write the word beginning with **l**. ....

83 Can you use the picture to find the story?

Write out each story.

shewillbegoingonthenexttrain

....

hewenthorseridingeverymorning

....

howmanythingswereleftonthetable?

....

Iamgoingtothefarm

....

hedidn'tseethedogtakethedoll

....

thegirllikedtojumpintothesea

....

theyplayedwiththebatandball

....

INDEX

These are all the words in this book. The numbers tell you in which games the words appear. You may need this list when looking for a special word.

A

a	47, 70
about	61
ace	54
after	73
again	76
all	40
along	23
am	83
an	12, 60, 79
and	83
another	64
any	60, 79
apple	44
are	34
around	75
as	42
ask	77
asked	77
asks	77
at	1

B

back	58
bad	15
bag	16
ball	40, 47, 83
bat	1, 83
bay	32
be	10, 83
because	71
bed	20
been	52
before	73
bell	27
bent	26
best	25
big	8, 47
bird	63
bit	2
black	58
blue	68
boat	70
book	41
books	41
box	44, 47
boy	32, 69
bring	22
brother	64, 70
brothers	64
but	6
buy	82
by	45

C

cake	37, 39
call	40
came	39
can	12
cap	14
car	34, 47
cat	1, 47
chat	7
child	71
children	71
close	61
cold	49, 74
come	38, 72
comes	72
coming	72
cost	31
could	74
count	75
cow	35
cry	69
cup	10
cut	6

D

dad	47
day	32
dear	51
didn't	83
dig	8
dinner	80
dip	21
do	5
dog	44, 47, 83
doing	66
doll	88
door	52
down	60
draw	38
drum	17
dug	8
dust	38

E

each	79
ear	51
eat	50
egg	70
end	61, 71,
ever	60
every	60, 71, 83

F

face	54
fall	40
fan	12
far	34
farm	83
fast	62
fat	1
father	70
fed	20
fell	27
few	80
find	28
fine	43
first	63
fish	58
fit	2
five	36
fly	45
fold	49, 74
food	19
found	75
four	55
fox	44
friend	61, 70, 71
frog	56
from	56
fun	13

G

gave	58
girl	63, 70, 83
give	36, 70
gives	36
glad	15
glue	68
go	5
going	66, 83
good	19
got	4
green	52
gum	17
gun	13

H

had	15
happy	44, 59
has	42, 47, 70
hat	1, 7
have	58
hay	32
he	10, 48, 61, 83
head	61
hear	51, 71
heard	71
hen	8
her	46, 48, 70
here	46, 47, 48, 53, 57
hill	29, 30
him	30
his	30
hit	2
home	38
hop	11
horse	83
hot	4, 44
house	70
how	35, 83
hug	8
hum	17
hut	6

I

I	83
ice	61
if	3
ill	59
in	3, 70
into	83
is	3, 47
it	2, 3
its	3

J

jam	44
jar	34, 44
jet	9
jump	83
just	38

K

keep	52
kind	28, 75
know	35, 61

L

lace	54
lap	14
large	34
last	62
later	66
led	20
left	82, 83
lent	26
let	9
like	72
liked	83
likes	72
liking	72
lit	2
little	70
live	36
lives	70
log	23, 44
long	23
look	41
looked	41
looking	41
lose	61
lost	31
lot	4
love	72, 73
loves	72
loving	72

M

mad	15
made	81
make	37, 81
makes	37
man	12
many	60, 79, 83
map	14
may	32
me	10
meat	50
men	8
met	9
milk	81
mill	29
mind	28, 81
money	82
more	73
morning	83
most	31
mother	64
mothers	64
much	43
must	38
my	45, 47, 70

N

name	39
nest	25
net	9
never	60
new	80
next	83
nice	61
night	80
nine	43
no	5
not	4
nothing	65, 79
now	35, 61

O

old	49
on	47, 83
other	64
others	64
our	55, 56
out	56, 61
over	73
own	60

P

pat	1
paw	38
pen	8
people	78
pet	9
picture	78
pig	8
place	54
played	83
please	70
poor	52
pretty	59
pup	10
put	6, 47

R

rabbit	78
race	54
rag	16
rain	76
ran	12
rat	1
reads	70
red	20
rest	25
riding	83
right	80
ring	22
road	78
roof	52
room	52
round	75
rug	8
run	13

S

sad	15, 59
said	56
sail	56
same	39
sat	1
saw	38
say	32
school	78
sea	83
seat	50
see	33, 83
sell	27
she	10, 48, 83
ship	21
shop	11
should	74
sing	22, 23
sister	70, 73
sit	2
sleep	52
so	5
some	38, 39
something	65, 79
song	23
soon	58
space	54
spoon	58
spot	44
stop	11
street	78
such	43
sun	13

T

table	47, 83
take	37, 83
takes	37
talk	62
tall	40
tap	14
teach	79
teacher	79
tell	27
that	7, 70
the	18, 47, 70, 83
them	18
then	18, 69
there	18, 46, 48, 53, 57
these	18
they	18, 48, 83
thin	65
thing	22, 65, 79
things	65, 83
think	65
thinks	65
this	18
those	18
thought	80
three	18, 33
through	80
till	29
time	82
tip	21
to	5, 70, 83
today	32
told	49
took	41
top	11
town	60
toy	32, 69
train	76, 83
tree	33, 47
true	68
try	69
twenty	81
two	81

U

under	47, 81
until	81
up	10
use	71

V

van	12
very	71

W

wag	16
walk	62
wall	40
want	77
wanted	77
wants	77
was	42
water	66
we	10
week	82
well	27
went	26, 83
were	57, 66, 83
west	25
wet	9
what	7
when	69
where	46, 47, 53, 57, 66
which	67
while	67
whip	21
white	66
who	5, 67
why	45, 67
will	24, 29, 83
wing	22
winner	80
wish	24, 58
with	24, 83
wood	19
word	62
work	62, 77
worked	77
works	77
would	74
write	66

Y

year	51
yes	43
yet	43
you	71
your	55, 71